Thomas McGee

The Irish position in British and in Republican North America

Thomas McGee

The Irish position in British and in Republican North America

ISBN/EAN: 9783337126001

Printed in Europe, USA, Canada, Australia, Japan

Cover: Foto ©ninafisch / pixelio.de

More available books at **www.hansebooks.com**

THE IRISH POSITION

IN

BRITISH AND IN REPUBLICAN NORTH AMERICA

A LETTER

TO THE

EDITORS OF THE IRISH PRESS

IRRESPECTIVE OF PARTY.

BY THE HON. THOMAS D'ARCY M^cGEE

Minister of Agriculture and Emigration, Canada.

SECOND EDITION.

MONTREAL:

M. LONGMOORE & CO., PRINTING HOUSE, 67 GREAT ST. JAMES STREET.

1866.

ADVERTISEMENT.

Many friends have desired to have this letter in a more convenient shape, than the newspaper form in which it first appeared, a fortnight ago, and I have great pleasure in complying with their wishes.

Some short notes on the antecedents of the Irish in British America will be found in the Appendix. The subject would bear very considerable amplification.

T. D. M.

Montreal, St. Patrick's Day, 1866.

LETTER.

MONTREAL, 3rd March, 1866.

GENTLEMEN :

If I venture to address the following paragraphs to your attention as a body, irrespective of party, I do so in the fullest confidence, that whether you agree with me in part, or in whole, or not at all, you are at least all equally disposed to give to a respectful statement, over a responsible name, a fair and candid consideration.

In what I have to say, I own at once I bear the testimony of a minority only of the Irish in North America. But the minority with whom my views coincide is not so small as some here and in Ireland may imagine. Many are silent from a constitutional distaste of controversy—many from a weak desire for their own personal ease and tranquillity—many from downright disgust of all things Irish, of a polemical sort. But our minority includes in its numerous ranks, so far as I know, all the Catholic Bishops, and a vast majority of the Priests of Irish origin in North Ame-

rica ; includes a majority of all our well-to-do settled
agriculturists ; our men of business, and professional
men ; includes all the influential and wealthy Irish
Protestant population ; includes almost all, I ob-
serve, of those who have won on this side the Atlantic any distinction in literary or politico-literary pursuits. The voice of such a minority, not rashly
raised, will not, I am satisfied, be lightly regarded;
and of this voice, I dare to assert, I shall be found in
this letter the faithful interpreter.

The chief obstacle to the true understanding of the
Irish position in America, Republican or British,
which I found last year in Ireland, arose from an ex-
cessive attachment to preconceived opinions. Men
who had never seen a sun rise and set on the Atlantic, much less on the world beyond, had framed for
themselves a fancy picture of this continent, and
were prepared to swear it was the only true likeness.
Their notions were like those of that gifted daughter
of the gifted house of Sheridan, who makes her emi-
grant declare that when he reaches America he will
sit and sigh away his hours, with closed eyes, in our
" grand old woods." If he did so in some of them,
he would need to carry a charm, or he might find a
garter snake about his legs and the mosquitoes about
his ears before he was seated in the "grand old
woods" many minutes. In the same way all our
trans-Atlantic visitors are, at first sight, disappointed

with Niagara; for stupendous as nature is in that place, the soaring imagination of man overtops and looks down on all material grandeur. The cataract, the snake or the mosquito, displaces by actual contact preconceived opinions, and substitutes simple realities. I cannot hope that any words of mine should dispel mental or moral Niagaras, but the understanding must be deranged indeed, to which the words of truth and earnestness cannot convey conviction, as readily as the sting of an insect or the venom of a reptile conveys pain to the body.

Of the erroneous impressions existing in Ireland, alike as to Republican and British America, it must be owned the main source is a want of downright candor on the part of the Irish on this side, in their communications with their friends "at home." To give pleasure instead of pain—to keep up heart and hope in anxious relatives and friends—to dazzle the neighbours—to enjoy a triumph even in their absence—the worst fortune has been made to appear better, the middling lot has been puffed into a prodigious run of luck, and even the best success has been exaggerated beyond bounds. I remember one of our countrymen in Boston about twenty years ago writing to his friends that he inhabited a four-storied house and drove his own carriage. So, indeed, he did; he inhabited the cellar, and drove a hack about town at a quarter dollar a fare!

If I have sinned against my countrymen in the States, as they are so constantly told by their misleaders, at all events it never was in this base way. I may have given many a sore shake to their fanciful and groundless self-satisfaction ; but if the truth, as I know it, is bitter, or if the relish for it is destroyed by a surfeit of stimulants, am I, therefore, to shirk my duty ? I would rather never raise a public voice, nor put pen to paper again, than betray them, and dishonor myself by such flagrant denials of the known truth, as, I grieve to say, are too common among them, when the subject is, their own position in Republican America.

This very Fenian organization in the United-States, what does it really prove, but that the Irish are still an alien population, camped but not settled in America, with foreign hopes and aspirations unshared by the people among whom they live ? If their new country was their true country, would they find time and money to spare in the construction of imaginary Republics beyond seas? If their leaders were real rulers at Washington, would they be playing at governments, think you, in Moffatt's pill-box ? * It is because the active spirits are conscious that, being Irish, they have no hopeful public career in the land of the " Know-Nothings," and the rank

---

* The " head-quarters" of the O'Mahony republic in New York, so-called from a notorious maker of patent-medicines who built it.

and file feel that while their stomachs are filled
their affections are starved in that hard and fast new
state of society, that all this weak and wicked yearn-
ing after the impossible has developed itself in both
classes. It is on the one part folly ; on the other
part crime ; but it is human nature after all ; at least
it is a new Irish-American variety of human nature.

There is a fundamental distinction to be drawn,
however, between those of our countrymen of whom
you hear so much at home, namely, the town, and
what I shall call the settled, well-ordered country,
Irish. Unfortunately for their own peace, and yours
and ours, the former bear the proportion of fully 75
per cent. to the whole. Causes, some natural and
justifiable enough—such as ready employment for
their labor on landing,—detained them at the great
seaports, or drew them to the factory and railway
centres. Never in the world's history, were a purely
agricultural population so suddenly and unpreparedly
converted into mere town laborers. They did not,
indeed, exchange agriculture for artificial pursuits,
for you cannot well call mere loading and unloading
ships, or porterage, or digging drains, or domestic
service, works of art. But the tens of thousands of
this class who were peasants in Ireland in the Spring,
and town laborers in America the same Summer.
threw up to the surface, by the natural law of their
numbers, a small fry of demagogues and overseers [or

" bosses"] whose interest it never was that they should look to dock and suburb labor only as a temporary condition, but to the acquisition and ownership of land as their ultimate object. Hence this strangely contradictory result, that a people who hungered and thirsted for land in Ireland, who struggled for conacre and cabin even to the shedding of blood, that this same people, when they reached a new world, in which a day's wages saved would purchase an acre of wild land in fee, wilfully concurred, under the lead of bad advisers, to sink into the condition of a miserable town tenantry, to whose squalor even European seaports can hardly present a parallel.

I described in outline the town Irish, high and low, [making, however, many honourable and required exceptions] in my speech at Wexford, in May 1865. Those whose minds were full of a fancy America, of course, could not admit that twenty years' experience enabled and authorized me to describe things as they are. Of course not! For us all, too often, Experience is the false, and Imagination the true guide. But the editors of the Irish press will not pooh ! pooh ! the testimony of the last Annual Report of the Metropolitan Police Commissioners of New York, which I take in a condensed form from the New York *Tribune* of January 20th, 1866. In this Report, the tenement house population of the Fourth and Sixth

Wards of that city, chiefly inhabited by our broken down poor people, are thus described. The *Tribune* says:

" The places are chiefly in cellars, with naked stone or brick walls, damp and decayed floors, without beds or bedding fit for human beings. They are mainly unventilated or lighted, except through the entrance door. In condition they are filthy and disgusting beyond description, overflowing with vermin and infested by rats.

" Into these hideous places are packed nightly an average of ten persons to each place, or six hundred in the aggregate.

" In violation of the laws of decency and morality, men, women and children, white and black, with no regard to the family relation, sleep promiscuously together, exhibiting less of the impulses of decency than the brute creation.

" From the character of these apartments, their owners and occupants, and the manner of their use, cleanliness is impossible, and hideous diseases of various classes and types are engendered and propagated.

" While thus occupied they cannot be made decent or healthy, and those who frequent them are beyond the reach of reform, except through the strong arm of the law."

Horrible details are then given of these general statements, and as showing the relation which your unhappy countrymen and women who have fallen into such hopeless servitude to the devil and his agents in the American seaports, bear to the proprietary class—the landlord class—in such cities as New York, I quote the *Tribune's* next statement, founded on the same Annual Report, which is in these words:

" It will be noticed, too, that many of these hideous dens are owned by ‘respectable citizens,’ officers in banks and the like, and are let out probably by agents —these citizens never taking the trouble to look at their property, and utterly regardless whether their tenants are poisoned or debauched, or in what way their houses affect the health and morals of the city. Surely, if any one sin needs preaching against by the clergy, it is this cruel neglect *by rich men of their tenantry, and their indifference to the condition of their dependents.*"

I suppose it will be a mortal offence against the pride and vanity of your America-makers, to show, on such authority, that so many of the Irish in New York city, the head-quarters of the two Republics, are still mere " tenantry" and " dependents"; that they dwell in " hideous dens," sometimes " six hundred" under one roof, " in violation of all the laws of decency and morality." Now, if these be facts— frightful as they are to contemplate,—what are we to think of those irrepressible patriots, whose love for Ireland is so ardent, that they are willing to cross the Lakes or the Atlantic to die for her, while they will not turn their steps aside down one of the dark lanes they pass daily on their walks where their countrymen and women perish by the hundred, body and soul! There *is* an Ireland enslaved; there *is* a battle for Ireland to be fought in the New World; there *is* a glorious, redeeming work to be done for her here; it is to be fought and wrought in the Fourth and Sixth Wards of New York, and in every large city south of the line, where our laboring population have suddenly been centralized, with all their old peasant habits stripped rudely off, and no new habits of discipline and self-government, as yet, substituted in their stead.

I say the *Tribune's* description, with some mitigations, holds true of our poorer people in all the large cities of the States; and the poor are the majority of the town Irish, who are 75 per cent. of the whole. But this horrible description of the New York *Tribune* does very rarely apply to the kindred population in our Provincial cities. Here, fortunately for themselves and for society at large, this perverted peasantry have not been concentrated so suddenly, or in such dense masses as in New York, Boston, and Philadelphia. Here, too, the leaders [for our race, like all others, will have leaders] have generally been gentlemen. In every British Province the foremost Irishmen have been among the first people in the

Judiciary, in politics, in commerce and in society.* This high standing has kept up the standard of the class, while, happily for us Catholics, the Church in these Provinces has always been sufficiently up with the people to preserve its legitimate control of their faith and morals. We are, however, but a tithe of our race in North America, and though we hold our own respectably and influentially with the rest of the Provincial population, it can hardly be expected that the example of 400,000 of us in the Provinces can bring about any radical correction in the conduct of 4,000,000 of Yankee Irish. I have great faith, for my part, in our steadily doing our duty by our own government, by our fellow-subjects, and by one another as Irishmen. I feel that we, at all events, have achieved a home and have a position to guard; I feel that we are in the right path; if we go on steadily in that path, good must come of it, for us and for all.

Let me give you an illustration drawn from this very spot, where 120,000 witnesses can vouch for what I state. We are " all told" in Montreal, men, women, and children, some 27,000 souls—Irish Catholics. At St. Patrick's, our principal church, between the middle of December and New Year's day

---

—thanks mainly to the good Redemptorist Fathers, —15,000 persons received holy communion, or very nearly every man and woman of an age to approach the Blessed Sacrament. Since New Year's we took up the project of building a St. Patrick's Hall, and during the first month $75,000 of the stock was subscribed, and above $10,000 of the first call promptly paid in! And these are the people, their own flesh and blood [though not of the same spirit], the New York " bloody sixth ward boys," are coming here to plunder, or, as they call it, " to liberate!"

Our rural numbers bear an almost inverse ratio to the urban, to what the same classes do to each other in the United States. I speak now of Canada. If not quite three-fourths, certainly the large majority of our emigrants in this Province now, live by land, and own land. There are at least thirty counties in Canada where the Irish Catholic vote ranges from a fifth to a third of the whole constituency, and in most of these, if the Irish Protestant and Catholic were taken altogether, they would form a clear majority of the whole. Persistent attempts have been made, and *greenbacks* have not been wanting to introduce the pest of Fenianism among our towns' people, but I am proud to say [with the single exception of Toronto] wholly without success. In Toronto one extreme is made auxiliary to the other; Orangeism has been made the pretext of Fenianism, and Fenianism is doing its best to justify and magnify Orangeism. Even in Toronto the brethren of sedition are a handful, and their Head Centre a nobody. Meanwhile the great healthful mass of the Irish farmers of Canada—men breathing pure air and living pure lives—are untouched by the infection, thanks to their own sound sense, to the inevitable conservatism which springs from property, and thanks too, whenever it is required, to the timely warnings of their loyal clergy!

The ignorance as to the United States in Ireland is only equalled by the ignorance as to Canada in the United States. There again the great obstacle to the reception of truth lies in preconceived opinions. The demagogical Irish leaders also, many of whom are glad to send their own sons and daughters to be educated in our higher moral atmosphere, have not the moral courage, or rather the common honesty, to tell the truth publicly as to this country. They know, right well they know, from personal observation, that the Irish *status* here is vastly higher than ever it was with them. But they find it more profitable to trade upon impulsive ignorance than to impart unpalatable instruction. They prefer to let their poor deluded followers believe of Canada what they have all along taught them, that neither freedom, nor justice, nor good government can exist under the British flag. Right well they know *we* have no State Church, no irresponsible territorial aristocracy, no proselytizing schools or colleges ; but they suffer their dupes to believe that Canada endures all the ills of which Ireland complains. Blinded by such falsehoods they would dash their reckless, homeless masses against this peaceful Province, which has done them no wrong, but where alone, in North America, their race has always had the fullest recognition. They do not see—fools that they are!—that they are still playing the game of " the Know-Nothings," who rejoiced two years ago over every butcher's bill coming up from Virginia, that, at all events, " the war would kill off the d——d Irish." There are a few more thousands, it seems, ready to be killed off, and your genuine " Know-Nothing " is quite content the Britishers should do it, so that he is not compromised in his trade or his foreign relations.

The game of mutual deception now played between "the Know-Nothing" and "the Fenian," is to the spectator, interested either in Ireland or America, utterly disgusting. The shrewd anti-Irish Yankee pats the Fenian on the back—urges him on to his own destruction,—and chuckles as he turns aside his head, at the verdure of his victim. The Fenian, on his part, who knows his gracious patron to be a bigot to the core, to be an absolute hater of everything Hibernian, pretends, in public, to see in him a genuine American, a real republican, a gushing lover of the entire Irish race ! Trying to deceive each other they fancy they deceive all the rest of the world ! Quite otherwise. The intelligent American regards them both with just as hearty a contempt, as any Englishman, or Canadian can ! He feels that the only practical result of a Fenian invasion of Canada, will be to make republicanism odious for this generation at least, throughout British America. He foresees that French Lower Canada, and Protestant Upper Canada, will alike revolt against an Irish travesty of Americanism, which, without the shadow of a pretext, breaks in upon their peaceful populations to destroy property in the name of progress, and murder unoffending frontier settlers, to the cry of *Vive la République* !

That the views I laid before my countrymen at home nine months ago, were not mine alone, I have since had many a proof from well-informed men, lay and clerical. But of all which has appeared, nothing equals in authority a recent letter on this subject from the Archbishop of Halifax to the Lieutenant-Governor of New Brunswick, which letter you, gentlemen, have most probably seen and reproduced. In that letter, with all the weight attaching to his station, his age, his powerful talents and sagacious judgment, the Archbishop points out the contrast between our two states of society ; and while doing generous justice to the United States, asserts for these

Provinces, as a home for Irishmen, a very decided superiority over the Republic. For this testimony against their falsehoods, Archbishop Connolly has been denounced by the Fenian brotherhood ; an additional proof, if any were wanting, that his views were founded on accurate observation, guided by sound principles of judgment.*

I did not, when in Ireland, gentlemen, and I do not now ask you to circulate these views and arguments in order to stimulate emigration from Ireland to British America. I say now, as I said then, " let every man who can live at home, stay at home." Too high a price · in body and soul may be paid for butcher's meat, and the wearing of glazed shoddy instead of honest frieze. If men, and women too, must sell their souls to the decent, well-dressed devil, who sets his man trap at the ship's side—well, of course they must. No advice will probably reach those who are ready to be so disposed of. But if among those who must emigrate somewhere there are some thousands left, who are neither dreamers nor dupes, but who can cheerfully encounter hard work, and joyfully obey good laws, then let them try Canada, or any other part of British America. Soon, with the blessing of God, British America will be one country, with one system of administration, and one wide field of enterprise and settlement. Four hundred thousand of your countrymen—nearly *two* millions of your co-religionists out of our total *four—*

---

* See Appendix B, for the Archbishop's letter.

are here to guarantee you a fair field and no *disfa-vour*—to guarantee your full civil and religious rights, not in theory only but in practice, not in name but in fact. Come, you who must emigrate, to us, and join with us in building up for our common descendants a free, an unaggressive, and a prosperous nation to the North of the St. Lawrence and the Lakes.

Such is all I have to say to the class that must emigrate. To those who can remain in Ireland, I will only add—beware of false intelligence from the United States. Never was the manufacture of false intelligence carried to such a pitch of perfection—if one may say so of such a business—as by those who make emigration a trade among our neighbors. Every flourish you see about the Irish republicans, read it backwards. You will be pretty safe if you obey this rule. As to Fenianism, it is folly in the mass, and knavery in the leaders, with very few exceptions. Do not remain (you who remain in your own land) pawns for speculators in Irish-American ignorance, to push about at will—remain to remedy the unhappy past by all reasonable and just reforms ; not as thieves in the night, conspiring for a chimerical republic, but as frank, fearless sons of the soil, manfully and lawfully contending that whatever is wrong shall be righted, and whatever is necessary to Ireland's peace and prosperity shall be supplied.

I have the honour to be,
Gentlemen of the Irish Press,
Very truly your friend,
THOS. D'ARCY McGEE.

APPENDIX A.

THE IRISH IN BRITISH AMERICA.

Newfoundland.—In the settlement of this Province
originally, the Roman Catholic Irish were interested,
since the first proprietors were Cecil Calvert, Lord
Baltimore, and his associates, who designed to draw
their cultivators largely from Ireland. In the reign
of Charles II. (1660-1685), they spent £30,000—an
enormous sum for that age,— in endeavoring to colo-
nize the peninsula of Avalon and district of Verulam,
afterwards Ferulam, now Ferryland. But it was not
till a century later, in the reign of George III., that
the success was granted to an obscurer name, which
was denied to Lord Baltimore. In the year 1753,
the total number of inhabitants was returned at 13,112
—Catholics (chiefly Irish), 4795; Protestants, 8,317.
But nearly half this total were summer residents,—
birds of passage, who flitted with the season. In 1784,
the Rev. Dr. O'Donnell, a Franciscan Friar, born in
Tipperary, and educated at Prague, availing himself
of the toleration in religion set forth in the royal
proclamation relating to Newfoundland, became, in
reality, the founder of the Irish settlements in the
Island. He was appointed in 1796, by the sainted

Pope Pius VI, first Bishop of the Island, and has had as successors Bishops Lambert, Scallan, Fleming, and the present learned and accomplished incumbent, Dr. Mullock. There is now a second Episcopal See— Harbor Grace. Strange as it may seem, Bishop O'Donnell's greatest difficulty was to induce the royal Admirals and Governors, of eighty years ago, *to permit* his flock to winter on the Island, instead of returning to Ireland or the American mainland. For his services in suppressing a mutiny among the troops under command of Colonel Skerret, this Bishop received a small annuity (£50 sterling for life], from the Imperial Government, and on resigning his See, in the 70th year of his age [1807], he was presented with a superb silver urn, with an appropriate inscription, which it was the privilege of the present writer to inspect, in possession of the Rev. Mr. O'Donnell, of Bradford, Yorkshire, [a nephew or grand-nephew of the Bishop], in 1865. Ever since Dr. O'Donnell's time, the Catholic Bishops have borne a very important part, not only in the moral government, but in the material advancement of the people. The 13,000 of a floating population in 1753, have become a fixed people of 130,000. The Irish Catholic laity have quite kept pace in education and influence with the increase of the Church.* Of these, we need only mention the Hon. L. O'Brien, who has been Administrator of the Province; Chief Justice Brady; the Hon. Mr. Kent, the former, and the Hon. Mr. Shea, the present Premier.

---

* Two Lectures on Newfoundland, by the Right Rev. Dr. Mullock. New York, J. Mullally. 1860.

Nova Scotia.—The Irish settlers in Nova Scotia are almost coeval with the foundation of Halifax—1753. In 1760, Halifax was described, in a cotemporary account still existing, as divided into Halifax proper, Irishtown, or the southern, and Dutchtown, or the northern suburbs. It had then some 3,000 inhabitants, "one third of whom were Irish, and many Roman Catholics."† In 1755, Charles Morris, President of the Charitable Irish Society, was appointed one of His Majesty's Council for the Province of Nova Scotia ; and the Catholic faith, though proscribed by statute, was tolerated by a "humane inconsistency" of the Governors. Abbé Maillard, and Abbé Bailley were the first missionaries within the English period of Acadian history, and in 1783 or '84 the first tolerated chapel was opened in Halifax, under the name of St. Peter's. For thirty years the highest Catholic authority was a Vicar-General to the Bishop of Quebec, until in 1818, the Rev. Edmund Burke, who had been a long time missionary among the Indians in Canada, was consecrated first Bishop of Halifax. This able, learned, and holy Prelate died, however, in 1820, and the See remained vacant for some years, until the appointment of Bishop Frazer, who was succeeded in 1842 by the late Bishop, afterwards Archbishop Walsh, who was, in turn, succeeded by the present eminent Archbishop, Dr. Connolly, in 1859. A large and prosperous colony of Presbyterians from the North of Ireland, in 1763, was commenced at Londonderry, and the next year, numbers of the same

---

† Letter to the Rev. Dr. Stiles, of Boston, in Mass. Hist. Coll., quoted in Haliburton's Nova Scotia, Vol. I.

people, expelled from New England, began to settle,
under the lead of Colonel Alexander McNutt and
others, in what was then the wilderness, but where
now are the thriving counties of Cumberland, Colchester, Hants, and Kings. These were reinforced
at the outbreak of the first American war by several
families of Irish loyalists, and at the close of the
second, by many military settlers, officers and men,
from regiments disbanded at Halifax. Taken together
with their Roman Catholic countrymen, the Presby-
terian Irish formed, at the first census in 1827, nearly
one-half the population; and the following figures
from the last census will show how steadily they
have retained their proportion :

Total population in 1861 . . . 330,859
Catholics 80,281
Colchester, Cumberland, Hants, and
Kings 75,788

A very large proportion of the first names in Nova
Scotia are either Protestant or Catholic Irish—such
as the Inglises, Cochrans, Heads, and Uniackes,
among the former; the Kavanaghs, Boyles, Tobins,
Kenneys, O'Connor Doyle, &c., &c., among the latter. Years before the Emancipation Act was passed
in England, Michael Kavanagh was, by connivance,
allowed to take his seat for Cape Breton, and Mr.
O'Connor Doyle was admitted to the Bar. In the
rolls of the old Irish Society it is pleasant to see the
names of Bishop Inglis and Bishop Burke side by
side, and this traditional good feeling still eminently

distinguishes the highly cultivated society of Halifax.*

New Brunswick and Prince Edward's Island.—The data in our possession at present is insufficient to enable us to give a correct notice of the Irish position in these Colonies; but we hope to supply this deficiency should the present pamphlet reach another edition. The same gratifying description which has been given of our kinsmen in Newfoundland and Nova Scotia, will then be found equally to apply to those of New Brunswick and Prince Edward's Island.

Canada.—The first Irishmen who made acquaintance with Canada were a detachment of the famous Hiberno-French Brigade, which covered itself with glory at Fontenoy, and which had the honor to follow the lead of Montcalm in the famous campaign of the years 1756-'57. Upon the transfer of this Province to Great Britain there was, for many years, no special inducement for Irish settlers to establish themselves here. Lower Canada was tenaciously, not to say exclusively French; while Upper Canada, when set off as a separate Province in 1791, was at first dedicated to the sole possession of U. E. Loyalists, and " German and other foreign Protestants." Under the Constitution of 1791, we find, however, in the Lower Province, the name of Edward O'Hara returned as Member for Gaspé, one of the twenty-one Counties into which Lower Canada was then divided.

---

* For the data used in the above brief sketch, I am indebted to William Walsh, Esq., Barrister, and John Compton, Esq., Editor of the *Evening Express*, Halifax, who worthily represent the younger generation of Nova Scotians, connected with Ireland by descent or consanguinity,

He was one of the founders of an Irish settlement in the district of Gaspé, where marked traces of the race may still be found; and it may be observed that from his first election in 1791 till this day, Lower Canada has never been without an Irish representation in its Legislative Councils.* The County of Leinster, with its townships of Wexford, Kilkenny and Kildare,—dating from the same period, would also seem to indicate the existence of Irish settlements on the north shore of the St. Lawrence, between Montreal and Three Rivers; but of these we are not able, at present, to give any detailed account.

It is not, however, much more than half a century ago since the Irish communities of Montreal and Quebec—the *nucleii* of their class in Lower Canada—began to be formed. In the first ten years of the century "Dillon's tavern" was the principal Inn or hotel at Montreal; and during the same decade, [1804] the present English Cathedral at Quebec was built by Mr. Cannon, an Irish Catholic from Newfoundland, originally of Wexford. In those days a mass was specially said for the Irish in one of the churches of Quebec; while at Montreal, first the Bonsecours, and subsequently the Recollet Church, was given up to their use, during certain hours on Sundays and holy days. In the war of 1812-'15, many of the Irish were honorably distinguished, and on the establishment of peace, a very marked increase in emi-

---

* The first "Provincial Judge" appointed for Gaspé, (in 1799) was Folix O'Hara, at a salary of £200 sterling. In the same year, among the subscribers to the "benevolence to His Majesty" for carrying on the war with France, we find the name of Judge O'Hara for £27.

gration from Ireland to Canada took place. The 12,434 passengers who arrived at Quebec in 1819 from the United Kingdom, Mr. Christie tells us in his *History* were "chiefly from Ireland"; and the same [we presume], may be inferred of the arrivals of 1820-'21-'22-'23, which averaged about 10,000 a, year. The construction of the Rideau and Lachine Canals gave ready employment to laborers and certain classes of mechanics, two-thirds of whom, it was computed, remained in the country. In the seven years ending 1825, the total number of arrivals amounted to 68,534, of which the most part are represented as "tradesmen, journeymen, and day laborers, living in the towns of Quebec and Montreal."* In the seven subsequent years the average arrivals greatly increased,—the extraordinary maximum of 50,000 being reached in 1831.

At the general election of 1820, among the new members returned were Austin Cuvillier and Michael O'Sullivan, for the County of Huntington. Mr. O'Sullivan was a Catholic, a member of the Montreal Bar, Counsel for the Seminary of St. Sulpice, and one of the first Presidents of the first St. Patrick's Society of this city. He was possessed of great abilities; learned, witty, eloquent, and, in those duelling times, what was scarcely less necessary, personally brave as a lion. He died Chief Justice of Lower Canada, leaving an every-way enviable reputation behind him.

In 1831 Dr. Daniel Tracey, editor of the Montreal

Vindicator, with M. Duvernay, editor of *La Minerve*, were committed to prison by order of the Legislative Council, for a libel on that body ; and though they applied to the King's Bench for the benefit of the writ of *Habeas Corpus*, they remained in prison till the prorogation. Dr. Tracey was an "advanced liberal" of the school of M. Papineau, with whom he became joint-candidate for the representation of Montreal in 1832, and was declared elected by a majority of *three* votes.* He did not, however, live to take his seat, having fallen a victim to the cholera soon after his election. He was succeeded in the conduct of the *Vindicator* by Dr. E. B. O'Callaghan, whose immense services to Colonial history will be gratefully remembered, when his Canadian politics as journalist and member for Yamaska, are totally forgotten.

Of the large immigration from Ireland into this Province, for the seven years ending 1832, the only rural settlements of note which remain, are to be found in the district of Quebec, in certain parishes of Mégantic, Lotbiniére, and Portneuf; in the district of Montreal at Saint Colombe, and in some of the townships on the Ottawa. A full moiety of the whole found their way into the United States, and the remainder bent their steps towards Peterboro', Douro, or the Talbot settlement in Upper Canada. The latter settlement derived its name from Colonel Thomas Talbot, brother of Lord Malahide, who had served in 1791 on the staff of General Simcoe, the

---

* During this election, which was hotly contested, a riot arose, in which three persons were shot down by the military, and two were severely wounded.

first governor and true founder of settlement in Upper Canada. Tired of a military life, at an early age, he obtained in 1803 a grant from the Crown equivalent to half a million acres, or twenty-eight townships, in the fertile peninsula of Upper Canada. For fifty years he personally superintended the sale and settlement of this vast district, leaving, indeed, very considerable wealth to his heirs, but leaving to the Province of Upper Canada 150,000 of its most prosperous yeomanry.* Of these a considerable proportion, over a third, were Colonel Talbot's countrymen, irrespective of creed ; but he was far from being a bigoted nationalist. Subsequently the settlement of the country upon the Otonabee was undertaken by the Hon. Peter Robinson, who drew largely on Ireland for his pioneers ; whose after success and conduct in no respect disappointed their far-seeing patron. In the rebellion of 1837-'8, according to the testimony of Chief Justice Robinson and Sir Allan McNab, they stood unanimously true to their country, as did, with very few exceptions, their compatriots in Lower Canada, thanks to their own good sense, and the salutary advices of Father Phelan of Montreal, and Father McMahon of Quebec.

In Upper Canada, in the second generation from its settlement, the educated Irish settlers, almost all Protestants in religion, though liberals in politics, began to exercise a potent influence. Though their Catholic countrymen, neither before the Union nor since, have found the Protestant majority disposed to

---

* Colonel Talbot died at London, C.W., Feb. 6th, 1853, aged about 80.

elect to Parliament men of *their* faith ; yet they have always had it in their power to throw a casting vote, between parties, as they exist. With their aid and by their own innate strength, Robert Baldwin became the first Premier under responsible government, Robert Baldwin Sullivan the first President of the Council, and Andrew Manahan, a Catholic, the first member for Kingston, under the Union, when Kingston was the Capital. The same influence strengthened the position of men like Mr. Blake, the late eminent Chancellor. It is true the Catholic minority in Upper Canada has many difficulties to contend with ; but it is also true that, as compared with their own co-religionists, either in Great Britain or the United States, they possess many privileges and blessings of which they can hardly be too careful.

We can say with truth as to the actual position of the Irish in this country. From a few groups of pioneers and tradesmen, fifty years ago, they have now grown into a great community, possessed of Churches, Schools, property, political power, and social consideration. The following very general analysis of the Canadian census, taken five years ago (1861), will show at a glance their distribution throughout Canada, and the position they have attained.

ABSTRACT of the Population of Canada, showing the number of Irish origin and the proportion of Catholics and non-Catholics, as taken from the Census of 1852 and 1861.

	Total Population.	Irish Origin.	Catholics.	Non Catholics.
UPPER CANADA, 1852......	952,004	176,267	167,965	784,309
1861......	1,396,091	191,231	258,141	1,137,950
Increase........	444,087	14,964	90,446	353,641
Total increase per cent during the whole period........	46.64	8.40	53.93	45.08
LOWER CANADA, 1852. ...	890,261	51,499	746,366	143,395
1861.....	1,111,566	50,337	943,253	168,313
Increase........	221,305	....	196,387	24,918
Decrease	....	11.62		
Total increase per cent during the whole period........	24.35	....	26.29	17.37
PROVINCE OF CANADA, 1852	1,842,265	227,766	914,831	927,704
1861	2,507,657	241,568	1,201,394	1,306,263
Increase........	665,392	13,802	286,513	378,559
Total increase per cent during the whole period........	36 11	6.05	31 31	40.80

APPENDIX B.

THE ARCHBISHOP OF HALIFAX ON THE IRISH IN BRITISH
AND IN REPUBLICAN AMERICA.

The following letter was lately addressed by the
Archbishop of Halifax to His Excellency the Lieute-
nant Governor of New Brunswick :—

Halifax, 18th December, 1865.

SIR,—Allow me on the part of Her Majesty's loyal
Roman Catholic subjects in these Lower Provinces,
emphatically to thank Your Excellency for your
recent speech, and the fearless and out-spoken manner in which you have so effectively expressed the
bare truth on our behalf.

From all the sources of information at my command, I am convinced, if the crisis come, that the
whole Roman Catholic population in this country
will yield to no other class in unwavering loyalty
and the unflinching performance of duty in the day
of trial. Apart from the allegiance which, as Church-
men, we owe to the constituted authorities, we have
here everything to lose and nothing whatever to gain
by a change, be it ever so luring in the distance.
What can any Government give that we have not

got? We have prosperity, law, order, peace, unmeasured liberty, the country secured against foreign foe, trade and commerce protected all over the world at an expense one sixth less per head than in the neighboring Republic, and a mere fraction as compared with the expenditure of any other country we know of. To exchange this condition with any other, would be suicidal madness, and the thinking, leading portion of our people, the portion that have anything to lose, are aware of the fact. They, like myself, have visited the United States from time to time, and have had ample data to guide them to the same conclusion. Catholics, no doubt, enjoy many advantages in that country (and it is a blessing for millions they have such a country as a refuge), but after the experience of twenty-four years in British America, it is my deep conviction that Catholics, taking into account their numbers and opportunities, are wealthier and happier—better Christians—and socially and politically more elevated here than there.

In New York, Maryland and Louisiana, there are many Catholics in the higher walks of life, but few are Irish or of Irish descent, and they owe their position to anything rather than to the political institutions of the country. For over eighty years, I have yet to learn that one President, Vice-President, or any member of the General Government at Washington, was a Catholic; and not more than two or three of that faith (as far as I could ascertain) have reached that Senatorial dignity, since the days of Charles Carroll of Carrollton.

Catholics have now no share in the Executive, no

seat in the Senate, and but very few members in the House of Representatives. Wherever a few Catholics appear in their State Legislatures, it is admitted that our people, according to numbers, are but feebly and inadequately represented. These numbers are variously estimated at from three to five millions—and deducting the cosmopolitan city of New York with its foreign population and foreign vote—deduct the Catholic cities of Baltimore, St. Louis and New Orleans, where the mass of the people have belonged to that faith from the beginning, and what progress have they made, what position do they now occupy as contrasted with ours in British America?

In Canada, New Brunswick, Nova Scotia, Newfoundland and Prince Edward Island, there has been no period since the days of emancipation, at which Catholics have not possessed that influence in the community to which their numbers and position fairly entitled them. The Legislature, the Executive Council, and the Bench, are as accessible to the Catholic as the Protestant, whilst men of vast wealth and the highest business and social standing in every city, from Montreal to St. John's, Newfoundland, are to be found among our ranks. In all these particulars, according to our numbers, we stand as a hundred to one when compared with our fellow religionists in the neighboring Republic. The mechanic, the laborer, and the servant may receive higher wages there than here, (of which, however, I have grave doubts,) but taxes, costs, and charges are as three to one. Besides the tax on the raw material, they pay five per cent, on the cloth in their coats, and the leather in their boots. They pay five per cent more for them as they pass from the hands of the tailor and shoe maker, and one per cent on the sale of each article. Tea, coffee, cotton and silk, tobacco, liquors, match boxes, writing paper, and manufactured articles of every description follow the same category, so that they are now beyond all comparison, the most heavily taxed people in the world. Another war (and who can say how soon it may come) will make taxation still more oppressive. It is true, indeed, that at present wages, the poor, with prudence and economy, can meet these accumulated charges, (and they will be fortunate if they continue in the same happy position), but it cannot be pretended for a moment that they have the same substantial comforts and as much to spend at the end of the year as the same classes in every part of the British America. I have seen thousands migrate from here and not one ever return with a fortune made, or even an humble competency secured for their declining years. I do not know half a dozen among seventy thousand of an Irish Catholic population in the city of Boston, whose business position is half as good or respectable as that of hundreds in Montreal or Quebec, or even in this small city.

Our people, therefore, have nothing to expect from change of any kind but increased taxation, diminished incomes, a decided fall in the social scale, the scathing contempt of their new rulers, as was ever the case in New England, and with these, perhaps the horrors of a devastating war. The great Government of the United States has nothing more tempting to offer : and what have we to expect from the so-called Fe-

c

nians that pitiable knot of knaves and fools, who
unable to degrade themselves, are doing all in their
power to add another Ballingarry to the history of
Ireland, and to make the condition of our poor country more deplorable than before.

On the occasion of my recent visit to the United
States, many of these poor deluded people talked as
flippantly and confidently of taking all British America in the course of this winter, and holding it as if
they already had the title deeds in their pockets. If
they come on the strength of their own resources, it
will be indeed a laughable *scare ;* and from what is
now occurring at New York, we may easily foresee the
glorious denouement. Two millions of Protestants
and eighteen hundred thousand Catholics, who have
mothers, wives and daughters—happy homes and free
altars, and a Government of their own choice—will
meet them as they would the freebooter and the
assassin, with knife in hand on the trail of his victim.
From their success we have nothing to expect but
bloodshed, rapine and anarchy, and the overthrow of
God's religion—for all this is inscribed on their banners. Table turning and rapperism, the rhapsodies
and extravagances of a moon struck brain, are to take
the place of the old religion in Ireland, and the
priests of the land are to be exterminated under the
fostering ægis of the new Republic. All British America is to be occupied and declared a neutral territory,
wherein Fenian armies and navies are to be recruited
and built up. The power of England is to be crushed.
Protestants, Catholic Priests, and the upper classes of
Catholics in Ireland are to be exterminated, and a

new republic is to be inaugurated with an ex-lunatic, Mr. O'Mahony, at its head ! With such a programme, the Catholics of this country will assuredly accord to the Fenians, if they come, the warm reception they so richly deserve. And, with prayer to the Prince of Peace, at this holy Christmas Season, and the earnest hope that they and we may be spared the trouble, I thank you again and again for your speech, and have the honor to remain,

> With sincerest respect and gratitude,
> Your obedient servant,

(Signed)   † THOMAS L. CONNOLLY,
Archbishop of Halifax.

To His Excellency
The Lieut. Governor of New Brunswick.

APPENDIX C.

St. Patrick's Day, 1866, in Montreal.

From the Montreal. Transcript, Monday, March 19.

Judging from Saturday, with the thousands forming the procession, with proud banners waving, and the still greater thousands of approving spectators of all denominations, we have the assurance that, no matter what may be the occasion—either the sunshine of peace, or the cloudy tempest of war—we, as Canadians and British subjects, may grow up together and eventually form one mighty tree, which nothing but the will of Him "who rideth upon the wings of the wind" can blow down.

The procession had nothing in itself that has not been often described; but it had this signification, that the thousands of Irishmen, confident of their moral strength, could march through the streets with their clergy, without. a military escort, fearing nothing. From their place of rendezvous they went to St. Patrick's Church. Long before the hour appointed for Divine Service, the Church was crowed with a large and most respectable congregation. Hundreds of the citizens had to go away unable to gain admittance. When the procession had entered, the Priest entered the sanctuary, and Father Dowd commenced the celebration of High Mass. The music was exquisite, and the Agnus Dei and Gloria in Excelsis, from Haydn's Twelfth Mass, were most beautifully performed.

After the Gospel the Rev. Father O'Farrell ascended the pulpit and delivered an able and eloquent discourse from the First Epistle of St. John, chap. v. verse 4: "This is the victory that overcometh the world, even our faith."

After a long historical retrospect, the Rev. Gentleman concluded as follows :

See that yours is not a dead faith, or only in certain doctrines, but practical, lively, obedient. This was the faith that enabled the saints to triumph over the world—that he hoped brought this large congregation to-day,—which gave them confidence and power,—which enabled them to keep everything good and noble in their hearts, and said to all, if we are not true to God and to our Country, we are no Catholics. They must follow the model of their patron saint, and be loyal and obedient to those set over them. He was certain they would hurl contempt on the minions who would call them disloyal. *Semper ubique fidelis*, was the motto long ago inscribed on their banners,—always faithful over all the world. The more they were Catholics, the more faithful would they be to the country that protected them. Those who raised up strife were not Catholics, for they were not acting up to the rules of their faith. The Catholic motto was, "For God and Our Country,"—the Church first, but the Country afterwards. If they loved their Maker, the more they would follow His precepts, and these taught them to be honest, faithful, and true. Loyalty was ever characteristic of the Irish people. It was for clinging to their chiefs, in days gone by, that Ireland had been most celebrated, and they must cling to their adopted country now, where their faith was protected, where they enjoyed the fullest civil and religious liberty—under whose laws they were safe and rested secure. He implored them to cling to their faith, and to practise what that faith taught. By all the olden ties, by all the dear memories connected with their fatherland, by all the precious teachings of the Catholic Church, he adjured his hearers openly and publicly to manifest their faithfulness and loyalty. Give the hand of fellowship to those not of our faith, and be at peace with them. Respect for others would make themselves respected; they would thus prove themselves true children of St. Patrick, God's blessing would be upon them, and peace and happiness here and hereafter would be their portion. He prayed the Almighty, through His blessed Son, to drive away every element of trouble and division, of strife and of discord—making the people of this land happy, prosperous, loving, and contented. The rev. preacher concluded with a beautiful and touching peroration.

The procession then re-formed in Lagauchetière street. and proceeded along Bleury to St. Catherine as far as St. Denis Street, returning by way of Notre Dame Street to the Place d'Armes. At about half-past one o'clock the procession reached the front of the St. Lawrence Hall. The window above the principal entrance was decorated with evergreens, with a British flag over it. Hon. Mr.

McGee and Lt.-Col. Devlin, President of the St. Patrick's Society, entered the hall, and shortly after His Excellency the Governor-General appeared at the window. He was saluted with three rousing cheers, and three cheers were then given for the Queen, the band of the Victoria Rifles playing "God save the Queen." The following members of his Staff were in attendance :—Denis Godley, Esq., Private Secretary; Lieut.-Colonel Hon. R. Monck, Military Secre, tary; Lieut. Colonel Irvine, A.D.C.; Captain Pemberton, A.D.C.; Captain Bytheson, of the Royal Navy; with Major-General Lindsay, &c., &c.

His Excellency then addressed the Society and those assembled as follows :—

Gentlemen.—As the representative of your Sovereign, I thank you for this exhibition of loyalty paid to me as her representative. I have reason to believe that the sentiments of my fellow-countrymen in Canada towards myself are of the most kindly description. (Cheers.) But I do not consider this magnificent demonstration as one of personal respect to myself. I accept it as an evidence on your part of loyalty to our gracious Sovereign, and of attachment to the institutions of our land; and further, as a protest on your part against the principles and designs of wicked men who would disgrace the name of Irishmen by their conduct, who have threatened to desecrate the day sacred to our National Patron Saint by a wanton attack upon this peaceful. prosperous, and happy community. (Cheers.) I am rejoiced to perceive, alike from the manner in which I have been received, and the reception accorded to the observations I have made, that I have not misinterpreted your feelings. (Cheers.) I have proof of the existence among yourselves of the sentiments to which I have given utterance in addressing you. (Cheers.) And I have proof not only that you hold these sentiments, but this farther proof, in the position held by the President of the Saint Patrick's Society as the commander of one of the finest corps of Volunteers in the country, (cheers,) that you give no mere barren assent to these principles, but are prepared, if need should come—which God forbid !—to back your opinions with your strong right hands. (Loud and continued cheering.)

After some cries for " McGee," the procession moved on, and His Excellency retired from the window, being again greeted with loud cheers as he withdrew.

The procession then went down to the corner of the Haymarket and Craig Street, where the St. Patrick's Hall is to be erected. A platform had been erected on the roof of one of the small buildings at present on the site of the Hall, for the use of the gentlemen whom it was intended should address the meeting.

In front of this the procession halted, when Mr. Devlin came forward and said :—As President of the St. Patrick's Society, it naturally devolved on him to speak first on the present occasion. He expressed his hearty congratulations at the demonstration which had taken place to-day. He believed it was the greatest that had ever been seen in the city within the memory of the oldest inhabitant. (Loud cheers.) And at the present moment, and with the difficulties entangling the country, the demonstration of to-day must necessarily have the most pleasing effect. (Cheers.) He was satisfied that every Irishman present felt as proud as he did at the manner in which everything had passed off, at the friendly and kindly way in which all had been conducted. He did not mean to make a speech. He was now talking to them from the roof of a venerable shanty occupied at present, besides himself, by His Worship the Mayor, the Hon. Member for Montreal West, and four Presidents of various National and Religious Societies. And it was pleasant to think that before twelve months were over, on this very site, would be erected a building, the results of our patriotism, and bearing the name of the Patron Saint of Old Ireland. (Great cheering.) It would be a building which would reflect credit on them all, and do honour to generations yet to come. (Cheers.) The plans were now in the course of preparation, and, before the 15th of April next, he expected without fail to see the workmen busily engaged in the construction of the building. (Loud cheers.) As he had said at the commencement, he did not mean to make a speech, for they would now have the pleasure of hearing some remarks from His Worship the Mayor, and he would therefore conclude by requesting them to give three hearty cheers for old Ireland.

This request having been gloriously responded to,

Henry Starnes, Esquire, (His Worship the Mayor) came forward and was received with great applause. After thanking the immense number of his fellow-citizens, in inviting him, as Chief

Magistrate of the City, to take such a prominent part in this demonstration, and congratulating them on the great success it had achieved, he referred to the splendid sermon which had been delivered by the preacher of the day, wherein Christian charity and brotherly love had been ably advocated, and the duties of faithful and loyal subjects most eloquently defined. (Loud cheers.) He next alluded to the speech of His Excellency the Governor General, who had endorsed the loyalty of the Irish in words of truth and ability rarely equalled. (Cheers.) Some of their fellow-citizens had been against having this procession, and spoke generally against gatherings of the kind. Now he was in favour of them entirely, and especially was he in favour of this demonstration at the present time. (Cheers.) With regard to the fears as to the result of it, all had now been dispelled; everything had gone off quietly, and the Irish of Montreal had reason to be proud of themselves. (Loud cheers.) He had the opportunity of watching the procession, as well as of taking a part in it, and he declared it to have been the largest and the best, and the most orderly conducted that ever met in the city. He represented to those present the folly and the foolishness of removing their deposits from the Savings' Bank. Where could they be more safe than in an Institution of which their Bishop had the control, and which was watched over and guarded by their Priests? (Loud cheering.) He was himself a Director of the City and District Savings' Bank, and he gave his word for it, they were perfectly safe in depositing their earnings there. By withdrawing their savings they did an immense deal of harm to the poor, for from the surplus interest upon them within the last five years, at least $40,000 had been distributed among the charitable institutions of the city. (Loud cheers.) He had never doubted the loyalty of the Irish towards the country of their adoption; the great turn-out of to-day proved it to a demonstration. His Worship alluded to the false rumors circulated as to their disaffection, and said they were like many other scandals, easily raised, but thoroughly untrue. (Cheers.) The Irishmen of Montreal were never more loyal and true than they were now, and the circulators of reports to the contrary were no men, and deserved to be hounded down. He would not detain them longer, as a far better speaker—the Hon. Mr. McGee—was to follow him; but he would say, in conclusion, that to-day would mark an era in the history of this country—showing that the first commercial city of Canada was loyal to the heart's core, and let who would attempt to invade it, they would meet with a warm reception, and the old flag would be stuck to for ever. (Prolonged cheering.)

Some remarks were also made by the Presidents of the St. Patrick's Benevolent Society and the St. John Baptiste, and other gentlemen, after which the following address was delivered by the Hon. Mr. McGee :—

Gentlemen,—I am commanded by His Excellency the Governor General to thank you, in his name, for the compliment you paid him in calling at his present residence, and the cheers and music with which you greeted him. I deliver myself of this message with great satisfaction, for I think it is quite as much to the honour of the four societies as to that of Lord Monck—the scene we have just witnessed in Great St. James Street. (Cheers.) It so happens, gentlemen, that this is the first St. Patrick's Day I have ever been in Montreal —as in all former years since I resided here, Parliament was called not later than February; and I may say I have observed this day's proceedings so far with great satisfaction. I am not, as you all know, an advocate for public processions of one class of citizens—even when that class is our own; yet I cannot but congratulate you on the spirit which has governed your movements this day. We first went, as was most proper and laudable, to return our thanks to Him to whom we owe that we are here to-day, and where we received, from the lips of His minister, an instruction on our duties as Christians and citizens, which I trust we will all long remember. (Cheers.) You next, on your tour of the city, went to pay your loyal homage to the representative of our Sovereign, the Governor General; and you are now here to receive from the Mayor of the city the gratifying acknowledgment, that Montreal looks upon you, not as step-children or as foreigners, but as children of her own household, whom she does not distinguish unfavourably from any of her other children. (Loud cheers.) His Worship the Mayor has a large family; pretty well up to 130,000 of us; what we call in Ireland "rather a heavy charge." But it is pleasant for him, and for us all, to know that we are all pretty well able to take care of ourselves, and the Irish part of us not less so than others. I have analyzed the census of Canada, taken in 1861, and I find the Irish Catholics by birth a fraction under 300,000, and the Irish Protestants a fraction over 378,000, or, taken together, in round numbers, 665,000—a large fourth of the whole population of the Province. I rejoice to find, too, that the counties in which our countrymen are most numerous are among the richest in the country—a plain proof that they have enriched Canada as much by their industry as they have fortified her by their numbers. I will take, as an illustration of this statement, our own city. A gentleman familiar with our municipal assessment rolls, has done me the favor to go over them, at my request, and to copy out the known Irish proprietors—Protestant and Catholic. He may have made some unavoidable omissions, but what he has done is sure work, and what does it show? Why, that the valuation of Irish Catholic property in this city—and the valuation is seldom in excess of the real worth,—amounts to the very handsome sum of $1,993,330, and the valuation of Irish Protestant property (so far as my friend could identify the names), $1,500,000; taken together, the assessed value of Irish property in Montreal amounts to nearly $3,500,000. (Cheers.) And, gentlemen, we have other possessions far exceeding in intrinsic value all material property. That noble Church (pointing to St. Patrick's), the Orphanage beyond, and the Refuge beside it, all the altars at which we pray, all the religious schools in which our children are taught—these are possessions which we will defend to death. Here, on this very spot, as has been already mentioned, we hope by this day twelvemonth to see our St. Patrick's Hall rising up *vis-a-vis* to St. Patrick's Church, and representing $100,000 of our surplus earnings. As to our Volunteers, I think we have shown to-day that we are not behind the rest of our fellow-citizens, and I am glad to be able to tell you that on Monday next we shall have, I believe, a still further addition to our loyal and gallant Volunteer defenders. How, also, do we stand towards our fellow citizens at large, in our municipal and political representation? Who represents Saint Ann's Ward? A worthy Irish Protestant Alderman, and two Irish Catholic Councillors, Mr. Rodden, Mr. McGauvran, and Mr. Donovan. Who represents (in part) the West and St. Lawrence Wards?—Mr. Devlin and Mr. Mullins—Irish Catholics. Who represents (in part) St. Antoine Ward? Mr. McCready, who owes his election in great part to the votes of the most influential and respectable inhabitants of the Ward, clergymen and members of other denominations, and who I am sure will not abuse the confidence placed in him. Who represents the Victoria Division in the Legislative Council? Thomas Ryan, an Irish Catholic; and I believe you all know that it is an Irish Catholic that represents Montreal West. (Mr. McGee himself.) We are, moreover, interested in all those monuments of French piety and French munificence—the foundations of Madame d'Youville, Madamoiselle Le Bert, and the illustrious Margaret Bourgeoys, the foundress of the Congregation of Notre Dame. (Loud cheers.) Why do I allude to these facts to-day? Because I know that wicked or credulous men have dared to say that this great industrious body of people—one-fourth of the whole city—with their four millions worth of property at stake, with all the rights, privileges, and advantages they possess, would not be found true to the city and the country, if a day of trial came. I say the honest man that believes such an assertion is a weak man, and the dishonest man who makes it is a scoundrel. (Loud cheers.) There is no stigma of sedition in our ranks, and just as jealously and zealously as Father Phelan, (God be merciful to him,) guarded the character and conduct of his flock, in the last great crisis of this country, just as watchful as Father Dowd and his *confrères* watch over their much larger flock at this moment. The Catholics are taught as a religious duty, to render unto Cæsar the things that are Cæsar's; and while we obey the teachings of the church—as I trust we all do cheerfully in Montreal,—we can never cease to be good subjects and good citizens. We assail no man, we war upon no country, but woe be to those who wantonly assail and make war upon us. (Loud cheers.) Their blood be upon their own heads, and on their immortal souls the everlasting responsibility. Gentlemen, one brief allusion to the memory we this day celebrate. It is not a day for revelling or ribald speeches; it is not a day for idle displays of brute force, or offensive demonstrations of any sort. Those who think it can be celebrated in any such way, short of sacrilege, know not what spirit they are of—they make for themselves a St. Patrick's day, without St. Patrick. What manner of man was he, whose eternal birthday we all turn out to signalize nearly fourteen centuries after his mortal death? A captive of the sword, torn violently from the land of his birth, sold into slavery, and condemned to the menial office of a swineherd, did he cherish an undying hatred against his persecutors and oppressors. Not so—not so. When he recovered his freedom, and was restored to his country, like a true disciple of the all-forgiving Master, he yearned for the salvation of the people who had enslaved him, and returned to the land of his captivity, to lead captivity captive. (Loud cheers.) This is the true lesson of St. Patrick's life ; his gospel was a gospel of peace, not of hatred ; he besought Heaven for his people, as the son of David did in Gabaon, that they might have understanding hearts, " to discern good from evil." Whoever celebrates this day in any different spirit to this, is no true son of St. Patrick—but a spurious spawn, a bastard breed, whose pretensions are a deadly insult to the legitimate children of the house. (Loud cheers.) I might follow our Apostle through every scene of his eventful life to illustrate the theory of his character, for still he manifests the same true character, whether herding swine, or dictating a code to Princes—but I must not detain you too long upon your feet.—You have already given five or six hours to your celebration, and you are no doubt anxious to disperse to your homes. Gentlemen, I thank you heartily for the patience with which you have listened to me, and I beg to renew my cordial congratulations on the satisfactory result of the day's proceedings. (Loud cheers).

THE CONCERT.

In the evening a Grand Concert was given in the City Hall, at which an immense number was present, amounting, we believe, to some 2000 persons. At eight o'clock the President (B. Devlin, Esq.,) entered the Hall, accompanied by the guests of the Society, amongst whom were the Hon. John A. Macdonald, Hon. Mr. McGee, Hon. Mr. Cartier, Hon. Mr. Campbell, Hon. Mr. Cockburn, C J. Brydges, Esq., and others. The Presidents of the various National Societies also occupied place on the platform. The President opened the proceedings by some congratulatory remarks on the great success attending the demonstration, and also on the prospect that next year they should celebrate this day in their own Hall. He also expressed his regret that—this being Saturday night, rendering it necessary that the programme should be completed before midnight—they could not expect addresses from their distinguished guests. At the conclusion of the President's remarks the programme was proceeded with, and thoroughly enjoyed by all present. Later in the evening Gen. Lindsay and staff made their appearance, and were conducted to the platform. In reply to continued calls, Hon. Mr. Macdonald and Mr.

McGee came forward and spoke briefly and in happy terms of the successful demonstration now coming to a close. On the completion of the programme, three cheers were called for, for Old Ireland, the Governor General, Hon. J. A. Macdonald, Hon. Mr. McGee, and the respected President of the Society, each of which were liberally responded to. The band then played the National Anthem, which was greeted by cheers sufficient to raise the roof from the Hall, after which the large audience dispersed.